OCT 2014

MIDLOTHIAN PUBLIC LIBRARY

3 1614 00166 3302

W9-BIG-881

MIDLOTHIAN
PUBLIC LIBRARY

RESPONSIBLE GUN OWNERSHIP

Big Game Hunting

By Richard F. Kozar

MIDLOTHIAN PUBLIC LIBRARY
14701 S. KENTON AVE.
MIDLOTHIAN, IL 60445

ELDORADO INK

Eldorado Ink
PO Box 100097
Pittsburgh, PA 15233
www.eldoradoink.com

Produced by OTTN Publishing, Stockton, New Jersey

Copyright © 2014 by Eldorado Ink. All rights reserved.
Printed and bound in the United States of America.

CPSIA compliance information: Batch#RGO2014-1.
For further information, contact Eldorado Ink at info@eldoradoink.com.

First printing

1 3 5 7 9 8 6 4 2

Library of Congress Cataloging-in-Publication Data

Kozar, Richard.
   Hunting big game in the United States / by Richard Kozar.
      pages cm
   Includes bibliographical references and index.
      ISBN 978-1-61900-047-6 (hc : alk. paper)
      ISBN 978-1-61900-053-7 (trade : alk. paper)
      ISBN 978-1-61900-059-9 (ebook : alk. paper)
   1. Big game hunting—United States. I. Title.
   SK41.K69 2014
   799.260973—dc23

                              2014000393

*For information about custom editions, special sales, or premiums,
please contact our special sales department at info@eldoradoink.com.*

Table of Contents

Chapter 1

Introduction

Our colonial forefathers would probably be amazed at the populations of some big game animals that now roam North America. While buffalo are no longer legal game, deer, black bear, elk, moose, and wild turkey are still available to hunt, with several of these species dramatically expanding their range in some cases despite the encroachment of man. And much of this growth has come in the past 40 years, thanks measurably to scientific game management and conservation practices.

Consider Pennsylvania, where the whitetail deer population was so low in the early 1900s that conservationists feared for the animal's very existence and actually transplanted dozens of deer from Michigan. Now, hunters harvest over 300,000 deer annually, with another 100,000 or so killed by vehicles on the Keystone State's highways.

In addition, for almost a decade Pennsylvania has maintained enough elk in several northern counties to sustain a yearly hunt, in which sportsmen routinely take some of the largest bulls in the United

States. The same upward population trend holds for black bear. Thirty years ago, 500 would've been an average recorded kill in Pennsylvania. Over the past several years, state hunters have harvested between 3,000 and 4,000 bruins each year, some weighing over 700 pounds, and it's barely newsworthy when wayward bears wander into the suburbs of Philadelphia, Pittsburgh, and other metropolitan areas. Meanwhile, at an estimated population of 400,000, wild turkeys are likely more common today than in Benjamin Franklin's time, and can be found in virtually every county in the state. In the early 1900s, by contrast, only a few thousand wild turkeys survived in small pockets of the state.

The bulk of these big game animals are today harvested by gun hunters, using rifles in most cases, along with shotguns and modern in-line muzzleloaders. This book will thus concentrate on firearm hunting exclusively, and is intended for novice hunters of any age. And although there are several species of big game such as bighorn sheep, mountain goats, and antelope that inhabit the more remote regions of the western United States, we're going to concentrate on the big game animals that the average hunter of modest means can pursue in his home state or within a reasonable drive.

USING THE RIGHT AMMUNITION

Rifles are classified by the *caliber*, or diameter, of the gun's bore and the bullet it fires. The smaller the caliber, the smaller the bullet. A bullet is a metal projectile, usually lead that has been coated with another metal, that rests inside a brass shell loaded with smokeless gunpowder and a primer. (This is known as a cartridge.) When a hunter pulls the trigger, the firing pin in his firearm hits the primer in the cartridge, causing a mini-explosion that propels the bullet through the bore and toward its target.

A bullet can either be fired from a relatively low-velocity, non-reusable rimfire cartridge (such as a .22 caliber, typically used for plinking at targets or hunting small game) or centerfire cartridges, which contain more powder, propel the bullet at a higher velocity, and can be reloaded by home hobbyists. Centerfire cartridges are required

Responsible hunters play an important role in controlling game populations. State wildlife agencies manage their hunting seasons so that the number of bears, deer, elk, and other large game are maintained at a level that can be sustained within the area where these animals make their homes.

for big game hunting because they have enough power to almost guarantee a kill if you hit your target in a vital area. Responsible hunters always try to harvest animals cleanly, not leave them wounded and able to wander away to suffer and die in the woods. Each chapter of this book will include information on the proper ammunition cartridges to use when hunting that particular game.

Bullets are measured in weight by grains (110, 130, 150, 180, etc.) The heavier the grain, the heavier the bullet. Generally, bigger grain bullets are recommended for larger game animals because of the punch they deliver. If a hunter uses a bullet that is too light—for example, 120 grains for a moose—it may not deliver the lethal impact

Elk, deer, and other big game have sensitive noses, so hunting into the wind is essential if you want to get close for a good shot.

required. Conversely, a heavier grain bullet hitting a smaller animal basically amounts to overkill. Acceptable bullet weights for deer are 130-grain to 150-grain. For beer, elk, and moose, follow the recommended bullet weights listed in each chapter.

In general, it's a good idea to hunt big game with premium controlled expanding bullets. Basically, these bullets are factory loaded under tight tolerances to assure reliability. In addition, the projectiles—of lead, zinc, and copper alloys—are designed to expand relatively quickly upon impact, yet maintain most of their mass, all the while penetrating deeply enough into a big game animal to assure maximum tissue damage and knockdown power. It's a tall order for an individual bullet, but several manufactures do deliver on the promise of an all-around exceptional product. Read online reviews to discover which brands are best for the cartridge size you need.

AFTER THE KILL

Once you've killed a big game animal, it's often said that "the fun's just begun." That's because your next task is to field dress it, and decide how to remove it from the area. Turkeys are a cakewalk compared to other big game simply because they're not that big. You can easily field dress a gobbler or hen by making a horizontal incision either side of the anus and then reach in to pull out the intestines, heart/lungs, and gizzard. Not every hunter bothers with field-dressing a turkey, but bacteria begins to work on internal organs minutes after an animal dies, meaning there's a chance the surrounding meat will spoil, especially if the weather's warm. The faster you cool down an animal's internal temperature, the less chance meat will spoil.

When it comes to deer, bear, elk, and moose, you absolutely have to field-dress them as soon as possible. First, roll the animal on its back, propping if necessary. Now make an incision through its hide, starting at the breast bone and working back to the genitals. Next, make a small second cut through the muscle tissue, insert two fingers as a knife guide, lift the belly muscle slightly, and proceed to cut back to the genitals. This way you won't puncture internal organs or the intestines. You'll also make a circular cut around the anus, after which you'll withdraw the large intestine and urethra into the body cavity for removal, taking care not to drop urine or feces in the animal. Roll it on its side, then pull out the intestines, making cuts to separate connective tissues as necessary. Now cut through the animal's diaphragm and remove the lungs, heart, and windpipe.

If your prize is a deer, you can simply tag it, tie its front legs to the head or antlers, and begin dragging it back to your vehicle using a pull rope. Same with a bear weighing 150 pounds (68 kilograms) or less. But with any larger game, especially elk and moose, the only choice is to skin the animal on site, separate the carcass into manageable portions, often called "quarters," and haul them out piecemeal. You'll probably need a bone saw, meat sacks, and a pack horse or back pack to accomplish this task. And however you do so, the meat must be allowed to cool as quickly as possible to prevent contamination. A bag of ice thrown into a deer or bear's chest cavity will help until you can reach a butcher. And presuming the air temperature is 40° Fahrenheit (4° Celsius) or less, the quarters and meat can be hung outside until you reach a meat processor. Otherwise, the trophy you worked so hard to bag may provide meat that's distasteful at best and dangerous to consume at worst.

Using Telescopic Sights

Binoculars and telescopic sights—or scopes—give big game hunters a clear advantage when an animal is far away or standing in thick cover. For instance, you might not be able to determine by sight if a group of deer includes a buck, and whether he has legal or even trophy antlers. This is where a binocular comes in handy. For safety's sake, always check out big game by binocular unless you're positive you're looking at an animal. Plus, binoculars often have a wider field of vision than most scopes, so you'll be able to more easily pick out animals with them. If glassing this way does help you single out an animal you'd consider shooting, switch to your rifle scope for closer inspection. Assuming your rifle is fitted with the variable power 2-7x scope we recommend, you can easily adjust it to home in on your prospective target. Each scope comes with an adjustment dial on the ocular

lens, or eyepiece, that you view through. The lower the power it's set on, the wider the field of vision, but the smaller your target will appear. As you increase the power by turning the dial, your target will be magnified and appear closer in the scope. However, your field of vision will decrease, so there's a trade-off between scoping an animal at lower power to pick it out and then increasing magnification when you place the crosshairs on a vital area for the shot.

Never use the scope on your rifle to scan an area for game. A basic safety rule is to only point a firearm at something you intend to kill. Bring a pair of binoculars to identify legal targets before you raise and aim your firearm.

One way to assure you will hit an animal's vitals, whether it's up close and personal or several hundred yards away, is to "zero" your scope. Attach a paper target purchased from a sporting goods store to a stump or sheet of plywood 25 yards away, with a safe backstop behind it such as a sand or dirt pile.

If possible, shoot from a bench rest where you can prop up your rifle for stability (sandbags work great). Wearing ear protectors, turn your scope to its highest power, view the target, chamber a shell, and squeeze off a shot. If you hit the bull's-eye, great. With this technique, using a .30.06 rifle firing a 150-grain bullet, you've just assured that your bullet will hit exactly at "zero" at 25 yards, not quite three inches high at 100 yards, and dead-on again

The scope should be about 3 inches (7.6 cm) from your eye, so that the rifle's recoil doesn't cause it to strike you.

at 250 yards. That's because projectiles like bullets travel in a slight but measurable arc over distance. As the bullet leaves the barrel it's rising, and will strike the bull's-eye dead-on at 25 yards. It reaches the highest point around 100 yards, which is why it'll strike nearly three inches above your aiming point, and why it'll also hit exactly where you're aiming as it descends at 250 yards. The point is, if you maintain a steady hold when aiming in the center of a deer's chest up close or 250 yards distant, with practice you can virtually assure your shot will hit it in the lungs or heart.

If your first practice shot is not in the bull's-eye, adjust your scope using the dials in its middle. The right dial usually changes windage, which determines your sighting adjustment left to right. The top dial changes elevation, or the sighting adjustment up and down. These adjustments typically are made in clicks, with each click moving your impact point by lower increments at close range and higher ones at greater distances. Since these adjustments vary scope to scope, read your operator's manual to learn how to zero in your scope if your rifle isn't shooting where you aim.

Chapter 2

Hunting Deer

Deer are the most popular game animal in the United States, by a landslide. A veteran outdoor writer once observed, "I can sell an article to any regional or national hunting magazine . . . as long as it's about deer."

When hunters think of deer in America, chances are they're picturing a whitetail, along with its various subspecies. This species of deer earned its name by virtue of the snow-white underside of its tail, which waves like a flag whenever the animal is frightened and fleeing. According to estimates, some 30 million whitetail deer inhabit the United States, and they are found in all 48 contiguous states. Texas has bragging rights for the most deer, at upwards of four million. Their range also includes much of Canada, along with Mexico, Latin America, and South America. A separate species known as mule deer—so named for their distinctively long ears—lives in the Rocky Mountains, Pacific Northwest, and desert Southwest.

What makes the current whitetail population astounding is that just a century ago, only about half a million deer were thought to live in the entire United States. In this modern age, where man builds

When startled or alarmed, the whitetail deer will flee, often lifting its tail to warn other deer that danger is nearby. In general, it's best not to shoot at a moving deer, unless you've already wounded the animal.

houses and commercial developments ever deeper into previously "wild" habitat, how have deer managed to not only survive, but thrive? Precisely because of man's intrusion. Each time humans clear the landscape of tall trees—whether it be for houses, farms, or airports—vegetation springs up that deer relish. (Unfortunately for homeowners, the "vegetation" often includes their expensive decorative shrubs and trees.)

Whitetails are primarily browsers, meaning they nibble on vegetation while they meander through woods, pastures, and crop fields. The list of things they won't devour is much smaller than the list of plants that they will eat, and deer have been known to strip all the edible vegetation from an area. One easy way to assess the health of a forest is observe the browse line: the maximum height a feeding deer can reach standing on its haunches. In areas where deer overpopulate their surroundings, the trees and shrubs of species they prefer are often devoid of leaves and branches up to six feet from the ground.

Deer also frequent orchards when apples and pears are ripening, and will take a heavy toll in soybean and corn fields, much to the ire of farmers. And when acorns and beechnuts drop, deer will gorge on these fall treats, even pawing through the snow to find them in midwinter.

Whitetail young are called fawns. They are typically born in the spring and weigh five to eight pounds. Fawns sport red coats speckled with white dots. By early fall, however, the spots disappear. Male fawns, referred to as bucks, are often slightly larger than sibling females, called does. They also have two nubs atop their heads known as buttons, the precursors to antlers they will begin growing the following spring.

When spring comes, a buck's antlers will begin sprouting from its head, covered by a coating called velvet. Antlers are the fastest growing tissue in the animal kingdom, but they are also soft, blood-filled appendages vulnerable to deformities caused by cuts, bruises, and insect bites.

A buck's antlers are fully developed by the end of August in most regions. The velvet will dry over the now-hardened bone beneath. To remove the dried velvet coating, deer will rub their antlers against small saplings or trees; this often removes bark and creates a visible

This large mule deer's antlers are bright red because it has just shed the velvet covering. Mule deer are typically found west of the Missouri River, particularly in the Rocky Mountains.

white tree scar that hunters will later seek when scouting for deer sign. A buck entering his second year may sport two single antlers called spikes or, depending on his local food and genetics, a thin rack with up to eight distinct points. Only after a buck reaches three years will energy devoted to growing its body be diverted to antler growth. The real wall-hangers of hunters' dreams are normally five to six years old. After this time antler growth peaks and often begins to diminish.

Whitetails have extraordinary senses compared to humans. A deer's sense of smell is so keen it can pinpoint a hunter upwind hundreds of yards away, just as it can easily detect the exact path of a sportsman hours after he walked through the woods and climbed a tree

stand to hunt. Their ears and eyes also miss nothing, particularly if a hunter betrays his presence by crunching through fall leaves or moving

Successful still-hunting requires patience—the slower you move, the more deer you are likely to see. Tread carefully to avoid breaking sticks or crunching gravel. Wear soft clothing, as materials like nylon will make a swishing noise as you move through brush. Stop often to look around and wait in position for a few minutes before moving again. Don't make sudden movements, as these will spook a deer (or any other big game you are stalking, for that matter). Always hunt into the wind; otherwise the deer will become aware of your scent and flee long before you are able to get into position for a good shot. Try to stay in the shade, as deer may notice the glare of sunlight off your face and clothing.

even the slightest when a deer walks by. The deer's only shortfall in senses is an inability to distinguish certain colors, such as the fluorescent orange most big game hunters are required to wear for safety.

By the time a whitetail is an adult, it will be almost six feet long from nose to tail, with a standing shoulder height of close to 40 inches. Bucks will vary in weight from 110 to 300 pounds, depending on age and region. (A general rule is that deer are lighter the closer they live to the equator, and heavier the farther they are away. For example, some of the largest specimens ever harvested came from northern habitats such as Maine, Minnesota, and the provinces of western Canada.) Does weigh less, between 90 and 200 pounds.

If hunters, especially novices, need one good reason to shoot only at standing deer, consider this: a whitetail can run 35 MPH over short distances, and leap an eight-foot fence when compelled. Consequently, few if any riflemen can humanely shoot a running deer with consistent success. Truth be told, the only time you should fire at a deer fleeing for its life is when it's already been wounded.

Otherwise, there's a very good chance you might never recover the very first doe or buck you decide to shoot. And that's a scenario every ethical hunter should avoid. For starters, if you cripple a deer with a shot through the stomach or intestines, it will likely go a long way, especially if you begin tracking it immediately. Second, even deer hit in the body don't always bleed enough for a novice to trail through dry leaves or dense undercover. Thus, if you're not very lucky, your quarry could run just long enough to be shot by another hunter or, worse, bed down somewhere it feels safe. If that's the case, not only will the animal likely die a lingering death, the meat will spoil quickly and feed woodland scavengers instead of you. So before you pull the trigger, make sure you're taking the best shot possible.

Which brings us to the choice of firearms. For over a century, hunters have debated—often heatedly—which is the perfect deer rifle. Young and first-time hunters are often initially encouraged to use smaller caliber rifles because they deliver less recoil, or kick, to the shooter's shoulder. However, such rifles also require greater accuracy when being fired because their penetration power isn't as strong as larger calibers. For example, a .243 bullet may not break a deer's front shoulder and continue penetrating into a vital organ such as a lung, while a .30-06 most likely would, even passing completely through the other shoulder. With that said, here is a list of rifle cartridges frequently used to deer hunt in the United States:

Caliber	Recoil (in foot-pounds)
.243	8.4
.30-30	11.4
7 x 57	12.2
.25-06	12.4
.308	14.8
.270	15.7
.280	16.2
.30-06	20.0
7mm Remington Magnum	24.3
.300 Winchester Magnum	27.2

So what is the perfect deer rifle? There is no such firearm. For while the .30-30 caliber of Winchester rifle fame is the most common, it is used exclusively in lever-action rifles and considered effective only up to 200 yards. Thus, it might appeal to someone pursuing deer in thick brush at close ranges but be impractical for a hunter in the wide-open Midwest who has to drop a buck 250 yards away.

Bolt-action rifles, which are chambered in all but .30-30 caliber, are the most accurate weapons a deer hunter can carry. And accuracy is crucial when attempting to put a deer on the ground as quickly as possible. Such rifles routinely come factory-fitted with open sights, meaning a shooter must align a rear and front sight on the gun barrel on the vitals of his target. With practice, many shooters can accurately hit a target at close range, say 50 yards or less. But beyond this distance, a telescopic sight mounted on the barrel is the best option.

Scopes are rated in powers of magnification. For example, a four-power scope magnifies an object four times. Most deer hunters will have all the magnification they need by relying on four- to eight-power

The best shots for beginning hunters come when the deer is broadside (left) or quartering away from the hunter (right). Aim at the rear of the front shoulder, as this area provides the greatest margin for error. A bullet that passes through the lungs and/or heart will typically bring down a deer, as will one that breaks the shoulder.

scopes. Scopes contain two intersecting lines commonly called crosshairs. All a shooter needs to do when sighting an animal is align the crosshairs in a vital area, and slowly squeeze the trigger.

What's a vital area? On a deer this is the lungs (which are just behind the front shoulders), the heart (directly below the shoulder), and to a much lesser degree the spine, neck, and head. Why? Because they are narrower targets, requiring pinpoint accuracy for a certain kill. In addition, hunters should wait for the perfect shot: a deer standing broadside, followed by one slightly quartering away and last and least, one quartering toward you. The point is to hit a deer where a bullet will have the most penetration through vital organs while simultaneously preserving meat quality.

As for other rifle types, there are lever-actions (such as the Winchester rifles used in Western movies), pump-action (portrayed by shotguns in just about any action movie), and single-shot rifles. Also extremely popular among hunters is the modern in-line muzzle-loading rifle, which uses a percussion cap to spark the powder behind a rifled bullet that's been ramrodded down a barrel a la Daniel Boone. While once considered a "primitive" weapon, in-line muzzleloaders nowadays can be fitted with scopes, making them as accurate as a high-powered rifle but only effective at shorter distances.

Last, some hunters choose to hunt deer relying on rifled, or grooved, slugs fired from shotguns. Such weapons in the bigger bores (especially 12 gauge) can also handily bring down deer, but again at more limited distances. The same is true for shotguns loaded with buckshot, typically a dozen or fewer heavy lead pellets. Slugs and buckshot are often the only projectiles permitted for sportsmen hunting in heavily populated areas where trees/brush are sparse and an errant high-powered bullet can be lethal to people several miles away.

Let's move on to hunting techniques. The most popular is stand hunting, or posting. It's a common opening-day technique throughout the northeastern states, where heavy hunting pressure gets deer moving at first light and hopefully keeps them on their feet all day long. One good bet is to pick a stand near a hilltop so you can easily survey the travel paths, or trails, paralleling the hill below. Some hunters prefer to ground hunt and simply lean back against a tree while waiting for deer. Others will take to the trees in portable stands, referred to as climbers (which hunters can shimmy up a tree in before settling in)

During the rut, whitetail bucks will battle for the right to breed does in estrus. You can attract bucks by simulating the sound of a fight. Using a pair of deer antlers, clash and rattle them together for about 60 to 90 seconds. You can enhance this with a call that mimics a buck's grunt. Then stop and wait for five minutes or so to see if a curious buck approaches.

Stand hunting is most effective early in the morning or late in the afternoon, when deer are moving between feeding and resting areas.

and lock-ons (which hunters hang only after using portable ladders to climb the tree or by screwing temporary "steps" that serve as a make-shift ladder.) Check game laws for the legality of hanging tree stands on public and private ground in states where you plan to hunt.

Another strategy is still-hunting into the wind, where you cover ground extremely slowly, taking no more than a step every minute or so while surveying your surroundings. Only the most patient hunter can still-hunt effectively, but it can be a great way to spot deer before they spot you, especially after rain or snow fall.

In certain parts of the United States, it's perfectly legal to hunt from ground blinds or tree stands overlooking food plots containing beans, white clover, or beets. In fact, hunters in vast Texas, where little public ground is available, often set up over electronic feeders that dispense food pellets to draw deer in close.

Elsewhere, however, hunters will up their odds of seeing deer by keying in on other readily available food sources, whether they be mast crops—acorns, beechnuts, and hazelnuts—or domestic crops, including corn and soybeans. In spring and summer, deer may feed in

If you hit a deer (or other big game) in the vitals, it probably won't run more than 100 yards (91 m). Be prepared to track an animal that runs away. Follow a blood trail, if there is one. Red, frothy blood means that your shot punctured a lung; darker blood means a less damaging wound. Be patient and persistent—responsible hunters make every effort to recover game they have hit.

crop fields throughout the day. But once fall approaches, and hunters begin prowling fields and woods, the deer become increasingly shy and revert to their true nocturnal nature. Then, the best times to intercept them are dawn and dusk, as they travel between food sources and their bedding, or resting, sites.

Routine goes out the window entirely during mating season, also known as the rut. At this time bucks begin sparring antlers with each other to establish breeding dominance, and eventually throw caution to the wind as the urge to reproduce overcomes their instinctive alertness.

When does come into estrus, or heat, it's not uncommon to see multiple bucks chasing them throughout the day for a chance to mate. However, many states don't schedule their rifle hunting seasons until the rut has ended. So if you are lucky enough to be sitting patiently in a tree stand when a mature buck cruises by looking for love, by all means whistle or imitate a deer grunt with your mouth to stop him, settle your sights just behind his front shoulder, and take what could be the shot of a lifetime.

Chapter 3

Hunting Black Bear

Centuries ago, *Ursus Americanus* probably inhabited every state in the Lower 48. Today, while its range has diminished, black bears may actually be more numerous than they were in our nation's early history. An estimated 300,000 black bears live in 37 of the 48 lower states, with another 200,000 in Alaska. Moreover, in several states their populations—as well as the sizes of individual bears—are climbing.

"Black bear hunting is better now than it has been at any point in recent history," explains Brian Bachman, founder and president of the North American Bear Foundation. "Conservation efforts and management programs have been very effective in restoring the black bear. Populations are increasing and ranges are being expanded in most areas. This is being reflected in record numbers of bears taken and also in the sizes of bears being harvested."

Wisconsin, California, and the state of Washington are each home to an estimated 30,000 bruins, and bears are legal big

These black bear tracks made in sandy soil near a river show the imprints of claws, toes, and footpads.

game in 28 states. In Pennsylvania, bear harvest totals have soared over the past 30 years, but it's the *size* of bears being killed in the Keystone State that has astonished observers across the hunting world. In 2011, for instance, Robert Christian of East Stroudsburg used a .30-06 to down a world-record black bear in Monroe County. Record-book bears earn their spot by skull measurements, not weight. Still, his specimen, estimated to be 10 years old, had an approximate live weight of 733 pounds.

Christian was deer hunting on a relative's property when the huge male approached him. Pennsylvania had a concurrent extended bear season in eastern PA, and Christian held a bear tag. He shot the bear four times after it appeared to be trailing an injured doe that had walked by him several minutes earlier. (Christian believed the deer had been struck by a car on a nearby highway.) It took two ATVs, pulling a trailer in tandem, to haul the bear out of the woods.

Yet his record-book blackie was just the latest in a series of giant bruins taken in Pennsylvania. In the Boone & Crockett trophy records for black bears, Pennsylvanians hold the second, third, fifth, sixth, and eighth spots of the top ten. Moreover, in 2009, the state game commission reported that 56 harvested bears weighed over 500 pounds, while in 2003 an 864-pound behemoth was taken in Pike County.

What accounts for the increasing population and size of Pennsylvania bears? Likely a combination of factors. First, the state closed its bear season for several years in the 1970s after poor harvests. This allowed the bear population to stabilize. Second, it instituted a bear license, which reduced the number of bear hunters by half. And last, the game commission trapped and transferred bears from traditional ranges to expand the population. Combine this with a diverse mix of available foods across the state, and you have an example of game management at its finest.

Let's focus now on black bear characteristics, habits, and how to successfully hunt them. First of all, black is not the only color phase they sport. While eastern bruins are indeed black well over 90 percent of the time, bears found out west are just the opposite: mostly brown, cinnamon, or blonde, at least in the Rockies and southwestern states. Biologists say temperature and terrain explain the variation. Bears that thrive in cool, deep forests with heavy shadows tend to be black because they blend in better with their surroundings. Lighter color phases, on the other hand, dominate in more arid regions of the U.S. because their coats attract less of the sun's heat. Furthermore, in northwestern British Columbia and southeastern Alaska, there are isolated populations of black bears with whitish to nearly blue coats,

The cinnamon variety of the American black bear is native to Colorado, New Mexico, Utah, Idaho, Montana, Washington, Wyoming, Alberta, and British Columbia.

Tree damage may be a sign that bears are nearby. Black bears like to rub against trees, scratch the trunks with their claws, and break off branches to feed on the fruit or berries.

because the colors blend so well with the bluish-gray glacial terrain they inhabit.

Bear cubs are born to sows at least three years old, with birth taking place in the middle of winter as the mother hibernates in a den or sheltered area. They will learn how to feed and survive by remaining with her until they are eighteen months old, at which time she'll abandon them and attempt to breed again.

A bear's vision is either as good as a human's or poorer over distance, depending on which source one reads. However, they do see in color, and have a sense of smell that may be unparalleled in the animal kingdom. There are documented reports of bears smelling humans from over a mile away and fleeing instantly.

Indeed, despite the occasional report of black bears being aggressive, they are far more likely to be shy and retiring, as long as they're well fed, uninjured, and don't perceive a threat to their cubs. And they are surprisingly nimble when startled, able to climb trees with ease and run up to 35 MPH over short distances. This is unexpected for an animal whose heavily muscled legs are designed for strength rather than speed, making them so-so predators of all but small animals and young fawns or calfs. Adults range in weight from 125 to 800 pounds, with males, or boars, being the heavyweights. However, the average bruin tips the scales at around 200 pounds.

In much of the United States, bears are denizens of the forest—either deciduous hardwoods found in the East or the dense pine forests familiar to Maine, Wisconsin, and Washington state. They can be spotted combing coastal beaches for shellfish, salmon, and other marine life, as well as high in the mountains up to 10,000 feet, where their diet consists of berries, nuts, and occasional dead elk or deer. If you want to find bears, seek them in thick cover; the thicker the better. These include alder patches, rhododendron tangles, recent clearcuts, and swamps.

Since bears are omnivores (animals that eat both plants and animals), the list of foods they eat is as varied as nature and man provide. In the spring, just out of their dens, expect to find bears grazing on fresh grasses like clover and the tender buds of hardwood trees. If a domestic beehive happens to be nearby, so much the better. Bears will not only gorge on the honey, they will also eat the larvae inside the hives and even the adult bees. Ant colonies are another favorite, especially ones in rotten logs. Surveys also show bears prey on deer fawns and moose and elk calves.

As summer progresses, they'll shift to whatever food is convenient, including blueberries, blackberries, wild grapes, and wild cherries. And when acorns, beechnuts and hickory nuts begin to drop, bears will sit on their haunches and pull the nuts closer with their front paws so they're more convenient to eat.

The same holds for farmers' crops. It's not uncommon in fall cornfields to discover a "crop circle" where a bear has pulled every stalk within reach and sat down to pick the cobs clean. Grain fields also attract them, especially oats. The same for fruit orchards, where bear sign ranges from busted limbs to claw marks and rubbed hair on tree trunks.

Man also feeds bears, whether intentionally or not. In springtime, bird feeders are a perennial attraction, as is pet food left outside. Refuse cans stuffed with food scraps are also convenient targets. In fact, bears will even dine on compost and manure piles in backyard gardens in search of calories, particularly in places where they have grown used to living near humans. That's why in states where bear populations are rising, so are the number of run-ins between man and bruin.

As in the case of deer, game managers have no other realistic way to control numbers than through hunting. And most bears harvested in this country are taken with firearms. While some hunters think a rifle suitable for deer is just fine for bear as well, there's no point in taking the chances of wounding an animal that sports much heavier muscles, bones, and sheer bulk. Thus, the rifles recommended for hunting black bear include calibers larger than a deer hunter requires, along with bullet size as measured in grains, or weight:

.284 Winchester (150 grain)
7mm Remington Magnum (150)
.264 Winchester (140)
.348 Winchester (200)
.308 Winchester (150-180)
7mm-08 Remington (120)
.270 Winchester (130-150)
.358 Winchester (200)
.30-06 Springfield (150-165)
.280 Remington (150)

Bear hunting regulations vary from state to state, including the seasons in which to do so. For instance, there is a fall and spring season in seven of the 28 states where bears are legal game. While not everyone approves of spring hunts because sows rearing cubs can be mistakenly shot, bears coats are in their prime then and the animals are typically on the move searching for food.

Tracking and treeing bears with hounds is legal in half the 28 states where bear hunts are conducted. One type of dog that is bred for this purpose is the Plott Hound; other hounds can also be trained to do this. One advantage of hunting over dogs is that a hunter can decide after a bear is treed whether it's a specimen he wants to shoot, especially if a knowledgeable friend or guide accompanies him. However, voters in other states, including California, have found the tradition "unsportsmanlike" and recently banned it.

Then there's baiting for bears, which is permitted in 10 of the 28 states. Typically, a hunter or guide places a bait "barrel," often a 55-gallon drum, in a known bear travel corridor several weeks before a planned hunt. The drums are then partially filled with everything from donuts and bread to fish scraps and roadkill, the more "aromatic" the better. Folks can debate the ethics of hunting over bait, but once again the technique gives hunters a chance to assess bear sex and size before pulling the trigger. Moreover, advocates say hunting over bait is no guarantee a bear will ever show up, and those that do tend to be ultra cautious before inspecting the attractants.

Next up is posting shooters along strategic points ahead of a group of "drivers," or walking hunters. In Pennsylvania, it's legal for up to 25 hunters to put on drives through bear hangouts, which include nearly impenetrable rhododendron and laurel thickets as well as clearcuts, areas where every tree has been harvested and heavy undergrowth regenerated. Bears frequently hide in such dense cover and might not normally be seen by a hunter if not roused from their refuges. The shooters often post on the game trails leading out of these thickets, and take a crack at bears as they come by.

Last is still-hunting, the technique of slowly covering terrain in search of game. Pre-season scouting is of the essence when still-hunting, whether one intends to traipse through a Maine clear-cut, hike and glass a Western ridge, or slip through an Eastern stand of red oak after a fresh snowfall. Bear hunting this way can be extremely productive, because bears' long-distance vision is forgiving and they're frankly not used to predators sneaking up on them.

And if you can't get to the bear, try luring the bear to you using a mouth-blown predator call imitating a rabbit or fawn in distress. Not every bear hearing it will respond, but all it takes is one desperate for an easy meal.

As with deer, the best shot is broadside to quartering away, aiming basically in the center of the chest. If you hit a shoulder first, so much the better; even a large black bear can't go far with a broken shoulder. And that is the main goal: downing a bear quickly, because their thick layers of fat inhibit bleeding and thus can make trailing a wounded animal difficult. Experts recommend using only premium controlled expanding bullets, which can mushroom to twice their factory size without fragmenting on impact, thus delivering the massive blow needed to down these magnificent animals.

Chapter 4

Hunting Elk

Few animals are more regal than elk, especially a mature bull with antlers so sweeping and wide they resemble a throne atop its head. The name elk is actually a misnomer: in Europe, it's the common word reserved for moose, which early settlers thought American elk resembled. Taking a different perspective, the native Shawnee and Cree tribes called elk *Wapiti*, meaning white rump.

Whatever you call this large member of the deer family, elk are part of America's heritage, providing meat, hides, and trinkets for Native Americans and early explorers. Lewis and Clark's journals from the Corps of Discovery indicate they shot 374 elk during their epic quest over the Rocky Mountains to the Pacific Coast in search of the fabled Northwest Passage. They tanned elk hides to make clothing and moccasins, and even as leather bindings to protect their journal pages. And young Native American males strung the upper two front teeth of elk, now called ivories, and wore them as symbols of long life.

Of the five big game animals discussed in this book, elk is one species that has shrunk in range and numbers since the Mayflower

The Roosevelt elk, pictured at left, tends to have smaller antlers than the Rocky Mountain elk (pictured on page 30).

landed in Plymouth, Massachusetts, in 1620. While an estimated 10 million elk once roamed vast stretches of the United States, including the East and South, their population is believed to be one-tenth of that now. Colorado has the largest elk population, estimated at 200,000, followed by Montana, Idaho, Oregon, Wyoming, Washington, Arizona, Utah, New Mexico, and California. Lesser numbers—but in some cases, huntable populations—inhabit Wisconsin, Michigan, Minnesota, Missouri, Pennsylvania, Arkansas, Kentucky, Tennessee, Virginia, and North Carolina.

ABOUT THE ELK

Four species of elk now live in America. Rocky Mountain elk carry the largest antlers and are the most widely distributed, including transplanted herds east of the Mississippi River. Roosevelt elk sport smaller headgear, but are the biggest in size. California is home to an elk known as Tule, which have the smallest bodies, while a subspecies of elk known as Manitoban inhabits the northern Great Plains.

An elk's coat changes color with the seasons. During spring, fall and winter, an adult's will be light brown, turning copper brown in summer. Hide of the head and neck is often darker, tending toward deep brown. A newborn spring calf, meanwhile, is camouflaged with white spots over a red coat at birth, and weighs about 35 pounds. As with fawn deer, they are believed to be scentless for several weeks and will instinctively lie motionless if predators threaten. Males are called bulls, and females cows. A mature bull of six-to-eight years will weigh 600 to 800 pounds; a cow about 500 pounds.

Unlike deer, elk prefer to graze primarily on grasses, as well as broad-leaf wild herbs and flowers. They will browse in winter on tender twigs and tree bark, particularly aspen. They've also been known to frequent mineral licks, which are sites where the soil contains naturally occurring salt deposits and other minerals. Many members of the deer family are drawn to these spots, biologists believe, to obtain essential minerals they may lack in their diet.

Bulls grow and shed their antlers yearly. These begin as long, skinny spikes, generally appearing in the second summer after their birth. With the proper nutrition, age, and genetics, these antlers will become the towering racks of hunters' dreams. Once they've shed velvet in late August, elk bulls will use their antlers to rub and slash trees, bushes, and the ground, attract cows and fight with other males, as well as defend themselves against cougars, wolves, coyotes, and bears.

Elk are casual herd animals, with cows and calves living together and bulls preferring solitude or bachelor groups. This holds true until

Never take a shot at a sky-lined animal, such as this bull Tule elk. If you miss your target, your bullet might injure a person that you can't see.

September, when the rut occurs and males sort out which will earn the right to breed cows, which the strongest bulls then herd into a harem. During this time of heightened sexual activity, bulls urinate on themselves while rolling in muddy pockets called wallows. Cows supposedly consider this scent to be elk cologne. And in a mating ritual for which elk are revered, bulls will begin bugling, bellowing eerie whistle notes culminating in a grunt. Elk communicate by vocalization all the time: calves squeal if threatened, and cows keep in touch with mews and chirps, and sound the alarm by barking. But during the rut, bulls bugle to both challenge other males and attract cows.

They also dictate their intention with body language. A nervous elk will raise its head, open eyes widely, and rotate ears to better gather sound. If a cow decides to go on a walkabout from a harem, the herd bull will circle her with an upraised neck and antlers tilted back. If they wish to threaten, they'll curl back their lips, hiss, and grind their teeth.

TO CALL OR NOT TO CALL

Modern-day hunters use the elk's propensity to call during the rut as a hunting tactic, one that Native Americans undoubtedly relied on for millennia. Consequently, sporting goods companies sell devices that imitate bull bugles and excited cow calls. Some hunters wouldn't think of heading into elk country without them. One reason is that elk territory is vast, sometimes mountainous, and often densely forested. In such challenging terrain, it's often difficult to figure out just where the elk are. And just as when hunting deer, elk aren't scattered everywhere, regardless how majestic the landscape. Like all game animals, they will be concentrated where food, water, and cover is available. Thus, hunters have historically tried to increase their odds of finding elk, especially bulls, by coaxing them into responding to artificial calls.

Not every elk expert thinks that's such a good idea nowadays, however. Some believe hunters should spend way more time pinpointing elk and little to none calling during the rut. Why? Because on public land where elk have been intensely hunted, more and more animals appear to have become what's known as "call shy."

A bull elk bugles as it walks through a river on a chilly morning during the rut. The typical bugle of the bull elk is a distinctive sound that starts out deep and resonant, and rises to a high pitched squeal before ending in a succession of grunts.

In an article published in *Field & Stream*, author E. Donnall Thomas Jr. recommends that hunters take the road-less-travelled approach to elk hunting. Bugling is overrated, he says, because hunters have educated elk by overdoing the calling strategy. He recommends calling only if you hear a bull and want to bring it close; not just out of boredom. "In doubt, stay silent," he advises.

Next, start your hunt finding where elk are hanging out before "stumbling up" a mountain. Then, once you discover their haunts, don't be afraid to set up a natural ground blind and try to ambush them as they travel from food and water to bedding sites. In lower terrains, they will often make feeding forays into hay, barley, and alfalfa fields, he says. Consider setting up a blind well before dawn on a game trail they use heading back from nighttime feeding areas. And next, don't "blunder into" bedding areas, or you will spook the elk so badly they may leave the area completely.

Also pay attention to wind direction, Thomas suggests, because elk rely on smell more so than sight and hearing. And if the wind's not cooperating, better to wait a day for it to change than push your luck and get busted. Because once you alert the lead cow in a herd, chances are you'll never see her or the elk with her anytime soon.

ELK HUNTING ON A BUDGET

Writer Randy Newberg had the budget elk hunter in mind when he penned an article for the Rocky Mountain Elk Federation. His premise is that an average person can hunt elk on public lands for $1,000 or less. He begins by pointing out that hunters shouldn't waste years hoping their names will be pulled in lottery drawings for "dream hunts" in prime elk country. Instead, he suggests you buy a readily available, over-the-counter tag in states such as Colorado and Idaho. Granted, you may have to hunt in the second or third rifle season or be limited to a cow tag, but this is a budget hunt after all. Besides, notes Newberg, cow tags are cheaper, more plentiful, and the meat tastes better than that from a bull.

By sharing travel costs with two other friends joining on the hunt, the trip becomes even cheaper. Along those lines, Newberg suggests bringing homemade, pre-cooked frozen meals, a tent for camping, and dry ice to keep any meat chilled in coolers on the way back. And yes, this means you and your pals will have to field dress, skin, and pack out your elk. Used pillow cases from a thrift store make perfect bags for the 300 or so pounds of meat an adult elk provides, he says. For even more savings, use the same clothing and equipment as you would on a deer hunt. Just don't scrimp on ammunition—buy premium cartridges, he advises.

Elk don't always maintain feeding and travel patterns as do deer, so be prepared to cover lots of ground when scouting. If that means hunting them in the hard-to-reach locales they seek out after the rut, then don't be afraid to head there; chances are you'll have little competition, especially in progressively later rifles seasons. Still-hunting is a proven technique in such situations, especially if there's snow and you take the time to sit and glass the surrounding countryside beforehand. In addition, take every step possible to reduce or eliminate your body scent. This includes using scentless soap and shampoo when bathing, and washing hunting gear in unscented laundry detergent. As for gear, the following rifles (using premium ammunition) are recommended:

.270 Winchester
.300 Winchester Magnum
.308 Winchester
.338 Winchester Magnum
.30-06 Springfield
7mm Remington Magnum

Once again, bolt-action rifles are considered the most accurate and dependable, especially mounted with a quality scope in 2-7x or 2.5-8x

Elk Hunting Gear

Because elk hunters tend to hunt in remote areas over difficult terrain, occasionally doing so on pack-horses, the amount of equipment they require can be extensive. Here's a suggested list of things to take:

license and elk permit	GPS
blaze-orange hat/vest	local topographical maps
two-way radio	rain gear
frame backpack	range finder
compass	emergency blanket
flashlight/batteries	game calls
insect repellent	waterproof matches
high-quality knife and sharpener	portable water containers

Elk tracks generally measure 3.5 to 5 inches (9 to 13 cm). When tracking elk, approach from above because they usually watch the downhill side.

variable power. However, semi-automatic rifles can be fired quickly and with less recoil, so they do have their proponents as well. As with other game animals, the trick is taking a shot while the elk is standing broadside or quartering away. Any shot that passes through both lungs will virtually guarantee the animal will collapse within 100 yards after being hit.

Finally, anyone hunting elk should be in good physical shape, as much for the hill-climbing required as the arduous task of packing out several hundred pounds of meat after the kill. Since elk hunts occur in early fall through winter, consider spending all of the summer building your strength and aerobic capacity. Depending on your age and physical condition, activities from mountain biking, trail running, and mountain climbing may be appropriate. If these aren't for you, at least consider starting a walking and hiking regimen, eventually graduating to a backpack filled with progressively greater weight.

If you have access to a YMCA or private gym, great. Explain your hunting goals to a qualified trainer who can teach you proper strength-training techniques on exercise machines or with free weights. Using a treadmill--especially while wearing a weighted backpack and walking on an adjustable incline--is a low-impact strategy to prep for the rigors of an elk hunt.

And if you don't want to spring for a gym membership, there are always the old standbys: push-ups, pull-ups, and sit-ups. However you intend to become fit, by all means do so. Your legs, back, and lungs will appreciate the training when you put them through their paces in pursuit of *Wapiti*.

Chapter 5

Hunting Moose

According to an ancient Arab proverb, a camel looks like a horse designed by a committee. The same has been said about a moose. For starters, the proportions seem all wrong. How do those spindly legs support its massive chest, head and antlers? Speaking of its head, what's up with its nose, which makes it look like some kind of cartoon character. The antlers—which can stretch as wide as six feet in monster bulls—make no sense whatsoever when you realize they have to maneuver them through spruce forests, alder thickets, and aspen groves so dense a person has difficulty walking through them. Nevertheless, moose have held their own in their home range, which is best described as the cool, wet North.

Granted, that home range has shrunk over the past centuries as hunting pressure all but wiped out the Canada moose subspecies in New England by the late 1800s. But conservation efforts, better land management, and the regression of farm land into forest have reversed that trend, and each year New Hampshire, Vermont, and Maine (with an estimated 76,000 moose) hold hunting seasons. In fact, for the past two decades moose have been creeping into parts of Massachusetts, upstate New York, and Connecticut. They also reside in northern Minnesota and Michigan's Upper Peninsula.

Another subspecies called Shiras moose exist in decent numbers in the Rocky Mountain states of Wyoming (7,000), Utah, Colorado, Montana, and Idaho. Regions of Oregon and Washington also support moose. But it's the Alaskan subspecies which stands head and shoulders above its peers in both size and population, estimated to be 200,000.

Moose are the largest member of the deer family, and reportedly earned their name from the Algonquin word *mons*, meaning "twig eater." It's an apt description, because they are partial to leaves and tips of white birch, quaking aspen, willow, and striped maple. They also dine on assorted wildflowers and aquatic plants, and have been observed nearly submerged trying to reach water lilies or pondweed. When nutrition is thin in winter, they will resort to stripping bark from trees, munching on balsam fir, and pawing through snow to nibble on moss and lichens. An adult moose can eat up to 70 pounds of vegetation a day.

Moose calves are born in spring. By the time they're adults, they can stand up to seven feet at the shoulder, considerably taller than an elk. Depending on species, bulls weigh 800 to 1,500 pounds, with cows 400 to 800. Only males grow antlers, which sprout in spring and expand rapidly under velvet over summer until the bone beneath hardens in fall. Moose antlers are unique in that they are palmated, rather than branched, with tines poking from the palms.

Moose tend to be loners rather than herd animals, although cows do watch over their calves with single-minded devotion. In the early fall, as the rut commences, bulls will start seeking out receptive cows, breeding as many as they can. Both sexes vocalize the mating urge, with bulls issuing grunts that can be heard hundreds of yards away and cows responding with a plaintive wail or moan.

Bulls will compete over cows, and aggressive sparring matches between rivals have been documented on film. Normally, the biggest bull with the largest antlers wins. This preoccupation with mating can also lead males to become belligerent with people. In fact, moose are

Moose like to feed in brushy lowlands. This clump of dwarf birch makes a tasty meal; other favorite foods are dogwood, willow, aspen, mountain ash, and aquatic plants.

responsible for more attacks on humans than bears and wolves combined. In addition, more than a few motorists in moose country have played chicken with a rutting male who refuses to give ground. Cows are also extremely protective of calves, and can kick behind like a mule and and deliver blows with forelegs like a boxer if threatened. They've been known to challenge winter hikers in Alaska who surprise them in alder thickets.

The biggest threats to moose are wolves, cougars, bears (black and grizzly), and man. Calves are most at risk from predators, but wolves in packs can run down adults when they're vulnerable in winter and harass them to the point of exhaustion.

It's in life or death situations such as these that a moose's long legs make perfect sense. Besides being formidable weapons against attack-

In winter, moose droppings will appear dry and hard. This reflects the type of things that moose eat at this time of year—twigs, branches, and other foods low in nutrients.

ers, they help the animals maneuver quite easily through up to three feet of snow. The wide hooves themselves act as mini snowshoes in winter and serve equally well when moose run through muddy bogs or swim effortlessly across rivers and lakes.

Some believe that moose have poor vision, but that may simply be a misconception. More likely, it's that, like a horse, the placement of their eyes on the sides of their head limits forward sight but gives them wide vision to the sides and rear, where danger would likely lurk in nature. Perhaps proving the poor-sight fallacy, one moose guide believed he spooked a bull hundreds of yards away simply because he silhouetted himself on a dock while walking to launch a boat.

As for the moose's sense of smell and hearing, those work just fine—a point hunters need to keep in mind when stalking or setting up stand locations. For example, since winds in North America typically blow out of the west, a hunter after moose would be foolhardy to watch a swamp from a stand located on the west side of the clearing. His body odor, regardless how well diluted with scent blockers, would drift downwind and spook any sensible moose. Thus, the east side of the swamp is the logical site from which to observe and hunt.

Many hunters pursue their sport from stands while waiting for a legal moose to walk by. The reason is simple. Moose live in dense deciduous or coniferous forests much of the time. Thus, the best chance to see one is in a clearing, including swamps, clear cuts, and power lines. For example, in Canada's province of Quebec, hunting just off a rural road is both legal and routinely done. In the fall season, residents park along gravel roads cutting through the "bush" and sit or stand, rifle in hand, while watching cleared power lines. Typically, they'll have trailered an ATV to help retrieve any moose they shoot. Hunting this way is popular because it's easy.

But not every hunter will want to sit in a treehouse or stand all day just waiting for a moose to show up. Nor will the local moose always oblige and make an appearance during daylight. This is the time it makes sense to go find the moose, and when pre-season scouting and in-season calling can pay off. Unless spooked, a bull tends to stay in his given territory even before the rut comes in. By scouting over the summer, a resident hunter can glass likely moose hangouts (like clear cuts in the Northeast) and determine which bulls are around. He'll have a decided advantage when hunting seasons finally opens.

And since moose will never be too far from water, look for them by boat in weedy back bays and exposed points along lake shores, particularly if an incoming or outgoing stream connects adjacent bodies of water. Moose use these low-lying areas as natural travel corridors

Moose are excellent swimmers, and are often found near water. These animals will not hesitate to cross a lake or even a fast-moving river in order to get away from danger.

because they are the paths of least resistance. Check sandy shores for tracks, droppings, and signs of feeding or antler rubs, and pay attention to any moose trails that terminate at water's edge. Many have been traveled for so long they appear to be moss-covered ditches through the northern landscape.

If you can't or don't intend to hunt from a stand, still-hunting is once again the natural alternative, especially if the moose aren't moving much, perhaps because of an untimely warm spell. If there's one condition that dampens their activity, especially during the rut, it's unseasonably warm weather. As a truly hot-blooded animal, moose are much like polar bears in that they prefer cool and downright cold weather. The reason is their dense hide and coats, which can cause them to overheat even in winter if the temperature rises above the low 20s.

A box stand like this one is ideal for moose hunting. The side walls will hide any movement that might spook a moose, while also providing some protection from wind and rain. You'll have the best chance of success if you set up a stand in the trees at the edge of a clearing, preferably near a bog or lake where the moose will come to feed and drink.

A canoe can enable you to navigate the areas where moose live.

And still-hunting doesn't have to be restricted to land. Hunting moose by canoe is an age-old strategy. It's a quiet, stealthy way to explore the kinds of backwater country moose prefer. Once you reach a clearing or beaver pond, that's the time to try calling. The key is to use the wind to your advantage, keep scent to a minimum, and employ the calls moose use during the rut and will respond to even after.

Since you have no idea how far away a bull may be, it's best to start calling softly at first, using a manufactured or birch bark call to imitate the low moans of a cow in heat. If you hear no response, wait a while before calling again, this time slightly louder. Only increase volume and excitement if you still get no response.

Your ears should warn you if a bull's succumbing to your calls. He may grunt in reply, or tip you off by snapping dead branches as he approaches. Don't be surprised if younger bulls are the first to respond. In nature, "teenagers" of many species respond quickest when the urge to breed compels them to act. If a bull does begin approaching, and it's a mature animal, it's not uncommon for it to hang up at some point and just wait. That's a sure sign it's either an old timer or one that's been spooked by calling hunters before. Now's the time to rely on additional calling tricks. You can imitate a bull grunt for starters, followed by slapping a stick or canoe paddle against

Aim below and a little behind the scapula, or shoulder blade. A properly placed shot in that area will pass through the heart and both lungs, which should quickly drop even the strongest moose. If you hit a moose and it runs away, allow 10 to 15 minutes before beginning to search for it. If the wounded moose is not immediately chased, it is more likely to lie down; by the time you get to the moose it may be unable to stand again and you can deliver the coup de grace.

nearby branches to mimic thrashing antlers. Last, if you're actually in water, convince him you're a urinating cow by pouring water out of a plastic milk jug into the lake or river. Sometimes these sounds are all it takes to make a bull come in close to investigate.

Because moose are so large and have unusually thick hides and bones, the smallest caliber rifles you should consider using are those chambered for .270 Winchester or .30-06 Springfield. Better choices are rifles chambered in 7mm Remington Magnum or .300 Winchester Magnum, using factory-loaded premium ammunition of at least 160 grains.

Bolt-action rifles are once again the most dependable firearms in clear weather or snowstorms. And unless you plan on shooting your trophy at 50 yards or less, by all means outfit the gun with a high-quality variable scope for the animal standing hundreds of yards away in a Maine clear cut.

Take only a high-percentage shot on a standing moose, preferably broadside. Use the crease behind the front shoulder as a guide. Aim several inches to the left of it, anywhere in mid chest, and you should drill a bullet through both lungs, which are massive in a moose. A few inches lower, and you'd hit the heart. Either way, by observing this time-tested rule you'll save yourself the heartbreak of wounding a trophy that can run as fast as a deer when spooked. For if your trophy moose dies a long way off and you manage to find him, you face the back-breaking task of hauling him piecemeal out of the bush even farther than you bargained.

Do yourself a favor long before the hunt and conduct some research. Check the harvest statistics of states you'd consider hunting, as well as hunter success percentages. In northern parts of New Hampshire, for instance, it's over 90 percent. Next, study topographical maps to pinpoint ideal moose cover in the areas you're considering hunting. Don't hesitate to use GoogleEarth to gain a bird's-eye view of the terrain. And by all means practice shooting live ammunition from an off-hand position, kneeling, and sitting. You can fire at paper targets at first, but consider rigging up a styrofoam or 3-D target that more closely resembles a moose. They are truly trophies of a lifetime, and deserve to be treated as such.

Chapter 6

Hunting Wild Turkey

No book on American big game animals would be complete without a chapter on the wild turkey, whose population today has rebounded nationwide to an estimated seven million. This figure is amazing when you consider that turkeys were nearly hunted to extinction by the time of the Great Depression. Our largest game bird inhabits 49 of the 50 states, and has even re-established ranges in several Canadian provinces.

Three-quarters of these birds consist of the Eastern subspecies, which reside east of the Mississippi River. Another million or so Rio Grande specimens call the central southern plains and West Coast home, while several hundred thousand Merriam turkeys live in the Rockies. Florida has its own subspecies, called Osceola, and a tiny population of birds known as Gould turkeys live in southern Arizona.

Like many birds of its gender, the male turkey, called a gobbler or tom, is a colorful chap, especially in the spring mating season. Its head becomes positively patriotic, turning shades of red, white, and blue depending on the intensity of the bird's mood. A gobbler's reflective feathers feature more colors than a rainbow: including bronze, copper, gold, black, red, and green. And all this feathered finery combined can put on quite a show. When trying to seduce hens, gobblers will fan their tail feathers, puff out those on the body, and drop their wings while performing a stiff-legged strut. Their chests also sport an adornment known as a beard, which resembles stiff hair bristles. Young toms, called jakes, might have a three- or four-inch beard; a two year old, a seven- to nine-inch one; and a mature three year old, up to a foot.

Meanwhile, the female, or hen, seems designed to blend in rather than stand out. Her coloration tends to dull brown, with a bluish-gray head, characteristics that may serve to camouflage her when sitting on a clutch of eggs or traveling with young chicks. Another way to distinguish gobblers from hens is by chest feathers: a hen's are tipped in buff, a gobbler's in black. Interestingly, two out of every 10 hens may sport a beard, although it's typically thinner and shorter than a tom's.

Eastern gobblers, among the biggest in the country, can weigh 15 to 25 pounds and stand four feet tall. Hens are considerably smaller, weighing eight to 10 pounds. Both sexes can run up to 25 mph when disturbed, and fly up to a quarter mile. Although they fly up to roost in trees at night and sail down the following morning, they are not flight birds in the traditional sense. Most of their travel is on foot.

Turkeys are omnivores, meaning they eat just about anything. Among animals they'll swallow are small snakes, lizards, salamanders, and frogs. Insects such as grasshoppers and crickets make up a large part of their diet, especially in early spring. As summer rolls around, they will shift to grasses, clover, and ripening berries. By fall, they'll have discovered where acorns, beech-, hazel- and hickory nuts lie, and leftover crop residue like beans and corn. After heavy snowfalls, they've been known to roost for days subsisting on tree buds. Thus, unlike deer, which can eat themselves out of food and cover, sizable flocks of turkeys can reside in a small area because their diet is so diverse.

In spring, birds will frequent gas wells, pastures, and fields. Although turkeys roost in nearby tall trees, they are drawn to open spaces in which to feed and breed. Without the handicap of dense foliage, the birds can see predators in time to evade them. And predators do take a toll on these birds, especially the young.

A tom struts before a potential mate, displaying its tail feathers. Male turkeys are looking for girlfriends in the spring season, which makes them vulnerable to a hunter able to mimic a hen's calls.

According to studies, half of the 10 or so eggs a hen will lay will not survive to hatch. Even then, assorted predators are a threat: including raccoons, skunks, foxes, coyotes, crows, ravens, hawks, owls, domestic dogs, and snakes of all varieties.

Luckily, the wild turkey comes equipped with keen senses of sight and hearing. Hunters often joke that if the birds could smell, they'd be nearly impossible to bag.

Thus, one cardinal rule of turkey hunting is never be caught moving. More hunters have been busted by moving than any other mistake. Turkeys have panoramic vision, and can detect the slightest twitch a camouflaged hunter makes. And their hearing is so acute an approaching gobbler can walk right up to a hunter who has called him in from several hundred yards away.

Which brings us to calling, the essence of turkey hunting. Turkeys rely on several dozen vocalizations to communicate with one another. Only a fraction of those calls matter to hunters, and most often in the spring or mating season. At this time, gobblers are as vulnerable as they'll be. Nevertheless, they don't lose all their wits. Spook one by moving or miscalling, and chances are he'll be twice as hard to fool the next time.

Here's a list of calls you'll want to practice before attempting to entice a spring gobbler. (Several web sites have recordings made of wild birds.):

Yelp—a series of notes turkeys make to communicate throughout the year. In spring, hens yelp to alert a gobbler to their presence.

Cluck—a short, distinct note to get the attention of another bird.

Cutt—a loud, sharp cluck made by an excited hen, often delivered in rapid succession. This sound can really fire up a nearby gobbler.

Purr—the soothing sound content turkeys make, often while feeding.

Gobble—the rolling rattle a tom delivers to announce his presence to rivals and attract hens. Remember, in nature the gobbler calls hens in to him, not the other way around. That's why drawing one within gun range using hen calls can be frustratingly difficult.

Putt—a single or series of sharp chirps. An alarm call meaning you're busted.

Kee-kee—a two-note whistle an adolescent bird makes, especially if separated from the flock in the fall. Often followed by squeaky yelp. "Where is everybody!"

Hunters have been mimicking these calls since Native Americans first pursued wild turkeys. For instance, an unknown ancestor discovered that a dried turkey wing bone could produce reasonable yelps when air was blown through its hollow interior. Thousands of years later, some traditional hunters still rely on this method.

However, when looking for more convenient alternatives, just peruse the manufactured calls sold by sporting goods stores across the country. You'll find hardwood box calls, where a hinged paddle is drawn over a three-sided chamber to produce yelps, clucks, purrs, and reasonable gobbles. Another choice among so-called "friction" devices is slate calls, where a thin, round drum is topped with a slice of slate, aluminum, ceramic, or glass. The caller uses a hardwood or synthetic stick called a striker to produce turkey talk by scraping it on the surface. These are especially good for making realistic yelps, clucks, cutts, and purrs.

Then there are diaphragm calls, a U-shaped, plastic-coated outer ring with latex stretched across it. When placed into the roof of a hunter's mouth and blown, diaphragms duplicate clucks, purrs, cutts, yelps, and even gobbles. Mastering them takes lots of practice, but they are the choice of expert callers.

Before hunting season opens in your chosen state, take time to scout the public or private land you intend to hunt (unless a guide or friend intends to do the legwork for you). In springtime, turkeys can be found everywhere from forested mountaintops and grassy glens to prairies and swamps. By daylight your best bet is to search fields and pastures where they perform breeding rituals. Wear full-body camouflage and head net, stay out of sight, and follow their progress through a binocular. And resist the temptation to call to them. More turkeys are educated by pre-season hunters than any other distraction.

You can also cruise country roads at dusk and pre-dawn, stopping periodically in hollows or valleys to locate birds. At this time, there's no harm in trying to get a gobbler to reveal its location by using loca-

A variety of devices are available that can mimic various turkey sounds and calls. Pictured here are (top left) a wooden box call; (right) slate disks and several strikers; and (left) several diaphragm calls (pink, yellow, and brown.)

The sit-and-wait method of hunting turkeys makes you harder for a tom to spot.

tor calls. In many parts of the country, hunters imitate barred owls, whose familiar hoots follow the cadence of "Who-cooks-for-you, who-cooks-for-you-all." This call can be made using a manufactured device or with your own voice. If a gobbler responds, you'll know his approximate roosting location, and can plan a hunt accordingly.

Assuming you have "roosted" a bird overnight, hit the woods close to an hour before sunrise the next morning and quietly sneak to within 100 yards or so of its location. While turkeys have limited night vision, they are not blind. The last thing you need is to blunder too close and flush your quarry, or other birds you didn't realize were nearby.

Sit back against a tree wider than your shoulders and taller than your head. Doing so eliminates your silhouette and ensures another hunter won't mistake you for a turkey and shoot you from behind, a regrettable hazard for spring hunters. Clear out any leaves or brush, rest your gun on your knees, and face where you believe the bird is roosting.

Once you've settled in, you can either owl hoot to trigger a gobble or imitate some soft "tree" yelps, which sleepy hens make on the roost. Don't turkey call loudly. With luck, your intended bird will gobble, and eventually fly down to search you out. Roosting birds are often farther away than they sound, while ones on the ground are often closer than you'd think.

Once a gobbler is definitely coming in, don't call any more than necessary. Oftentimes, he'll be more curious if you go silent. If the bird appears, he may be in full strut, a bad posture for a shot. Instead, wait until he his walking naturally, no more than 40 yards away and preferably closer. Your gun should be mounted ahead of time. Aim for the juncture of his neck and body, and take the shot.

A good all-around shotgun for turkey hunting will be 12 gauge, filled with #4 or #6 shot. If you've patterned your gun on a large paper target beforehand, you'll know how it shoots and what loads work best. Some hunters, including youths, may prefer a smaller 20 gauge for less recoil, but it should be loaded with three-inch magnum shells. Shotguns come in bolt-action, pump, double-barrel, and semi-automatic, and can even be fitted with rudimentary scopes.

One drawback to early spring turkey hunting is that a gobbler will often have a harem of hens roosting nearby. He may gobble his head off on the roost, but then button up after pitching down with the hens. Or he may continue to gobble to your calls but show no inclination to come your way. In fact, the hens may actually lead him away from you to eliminate possible competition. If a gobbler does pull this stunt, preserve your sanity—walk away and search out a more willing bird. But don't give up on him altogether if you still can't score. Return several hours later and either just listen, imitate a crow call, or yelp softly. The gobbler surrounded by hens that morning may now be abandoned and lonely as his girlfriends head to their nests. You may be surprised how easily he comes to you now.

We can't end this chapter without mentioning that colonial statesman Benjamin Franklin admired turkeys more than our national bird, the bald eagle, which he considered a lazy scavenger. On the other hand, he wrote his daughter: ". . . though a little vain and silly, [the turkey is] a Bird of Courage, and would not hesitate to attack a Grenadier of the British Guards who should presume to invade his Farm Yard with a red Coat on."

Organizations
to Contact

**Amateur Trapshooting
Association**
1105 East Broadway
P.O. Box 519
Sparta, IL 62286
Phone: (618) 449-2224
Fax: (866) 454-5198
Email: info@shootata.com
Website: www.shootata.com

Gun Owners of America
8001 Forbes Place, Suite 102
Springfield, VA 22151
Phone: (703) 321-8585
Fax: (703) 321-8408
Website: www.gunowners.org

**National Association of
Certified Firearms Instructors**
Tim Grant, President
4722 Forest Circle
Minnetonka, MN 55345
Phone: (952) 935-2414
Email: info@nacfi.us
Website: www.nacfi.us

National Rifle Association
11250 Waples Mill Road
Fairfax, VA 22030
Phone: (800) 672-3888
Fax: (703) 267-3989
Website: www.nra.org

**National Shooting Sports
Foundation**
Flintlock Ridge Office Center
11 Mile Hill Road
Newtown, CT 06470
Phone: (203) 426-1320
Fax: (203) 426-1087
Website: www.nssf.org

**National Skeet Shooting
Association / National
Sporting Clays Association**
5931 Roft Road
San Antonio, TX 78253
Phone: (800) 877-5338
Fax: (210) 688-3014
Website: www.nssa-nsca.org

Glossary

barrel—the long tubular part of a firearm, which provides direction and velocity for the bullet. The interior of a gun barrel is sometimes referred to as the bore.

bed—a place where a deer rests after feeding, usually indicated by grass, leaves, and dirt compressed in a kidney shape on the ground. Bedding areas are often surrounded by thick cover, but allow the deer to see and hear approaching danger.

blind—a device used to cover or camoflague hunters, to make it hard for game animals to detect them.

buck—an adult male deer, which grows antlers every year and then loses them after the mating season (rut) ends.

bull—term for an adult male elk.

bullet—the metal projectile expelled from the cartridge when a rifle is fired.

caliber—the diameter of the bore of a gun barrel, usually measured in tenths of an inch or in millimeters.

calling—the act of imitating the sounds that a big game animal makes in order to attract these animals to the hunter's area.

cartridge—ammunition consisting of a brass case, primer, smokeless powder, and a projectile.

droppings—the feces (scat) left by a game animal, which can be observed by hunters who are tracking wild game.

gauge—a unit of measurement used to express the bore diameter of a shotgun's barrel. The gauge is determined by the weight of a metal ball that fits in the firearm. For example, a ball that is one-twelfth of a pound would fit in a 12 gauge shotgun; a slightly larger ball that is one-tenth of a pound would fit in a 10 gauge shotgun.

mast—a food source of nuts produced by hardwood trees, such as oak acorns.

muzzle—the forward end of the barrel where the projectile exits.

omnivore—an animal that eats both plants and other animals for food.

rattling—a technique of calling whitetail deer by banging two pieces of deer horn together, which is meant to simulate the sound of two bucks fighting.

rifling—a series of spiral grooves cut into the bore of a gun barrel. Rifling stabilizes a bullet in flight by causing it to spin. Rifling may rotate to the right or left.

roost—a tree or other location where turkeys sleep at night out of reach of most predators.

rut—an annual period of sexual activity, occurring among deer, elk, moose, and some other mammals. During this time, males fight each other for the right to breed females.

scout—to explore possible hunt sites in order to gain knowledge of the area before hunting.

shooting zone—a safe direction in which to discharge a firearm.

stalking—the slow, silent pursuit of an animal, done until the hunter is close enough for a clear shot at his target.

stand hunting—also known as posting, this is a technique in which the hunter waits for game to come to him, often in a stand in the branches of a tree.

still hunting—the continuous, slow movement of a hunter through an animal's environment in hopes of finding game. The hunter takes cautious steps, stops often to survey the surroundings, and listens for the sound of game animals.

velvet—term for the soft growing antlers of a male deer, elk, or moose. When the antlers calcify and become hard in the late summer, the velvet falls off, or is rubbed off.

Further Reading

Airhart, Tom. *Elk Hunting Guide: Skills, Gear, and Insight*. Mechanicsburg, Pa.: Stackpole Books, 2013.

Bestul, Scott, and David Hurteau. *The Field & Stream Total Deer Hunter Manual: 301 Hunting Skills You Need*. San Francisco: Weldon Owen, 2013.

Combs, Richard. *Guide to Advanced Turkey Hunting: How to Call and Decoy Even Wary Boss Gobblers into Range*. New York: Skyhorse Publishing, 2012.

Etling, Kathy. *Hunting Bears: The Ultimate Guide to Hunting Black, Brown, Grizzly, and Polar Bears*. New York: Skyhorse Publishing, 2013.

Leghorn, Nick. *Getting Started with Firearms in the United States: A Complete Guide for Newbies*. New York: CreateSpace, 2012.

Lewis, Gary. *The Complete Guide to Hunting: Basic Techniques for Gun and Bow Hunters*. Minneapolis: Creative Publishing, 2008.

Nelson, Bruce L. *Hunting Big Whitetails: Tactics Guaranteed to Make You a More Successful Deer Hunter*. Fairbanks, Ak.: Buck Publishing, 2002.

Young, Jon. *Animal Tracking Basics*. Mechanicsburg, Pa.: Stackpole Books, 2007.

Internet Resources

http://www.boone-crockett.org

Boone and Crockett Club is an organization that promotes wildlife conservation and hunter safety. It was founded by Theodore Roosevelt in 1887, making it the oldest such organization in the United States.

http://www.nssf.org/safety

The National Shooting Sports Foundation's web page on firearm safety includes educational videos and articles about safe and responsible gun ownership.

http://www.nraila.org/gun-laws/state-laws.aspx

At this site, the National Rifle Association maintains a state-by-state listing of gun laws related to firearms ownership.

http://www.odcmp.com

The Civilian Marksmanship Program (CMP) is a government organization dedicated to training and educating Americans, particularly youths, about the responsible use of firearms.

http://www.nrainstructors.org/searchcourse.aspx

This searchable database enables you to find a certified NRA shooting and safety instructor in your local area.

Publisher's Note: The websites listed on this page were active at the time of publication. The publisher is not responsible for websites that have changed their address or discontinued operation since the date of publication. The publisher reviews and updates the websites each time the book is reprinted.

Index

Numbers in **bold italic** refer to captions.

About the Author

Richard Kozar is a freelance writer living in western Pennsylvania. The 56-year-old shot his first buck and turkey when he was 14, and has been hunting ever since. He has written articles for many publications, including *Salt Water Sportsman, Bowhunter,* and *Bowhunting Magazine.* He has also authored a dozen books for young readers, as well as *The Book of Chad,* the story of a young teen's battle with brain cancer.

PHOTO CREDITS: Warren Price Photography: 15; used under license from Shutterstock, Inc.: 5, 13, 19, 20, 22, 23 (left, center), 25, 26, 31 (center, left), 32, 33, 38, 39, 41, 43, 44, 49, 51, 58, cover; Nate Allred/Shutterstock: 10; Jeff Banke/ Shutterstock: 1, 48; Dennis Donohue/Shutterstock: 46; Dewayne Flowers/ Shutterstock: 16, 21, 54; Phillip W. Kirkland/Shutterstock: 11, 45; Julie Lubick/ Shutterstock: 35; Steve Oehlenschlager/Shutterstock: 14; Steve Price/Shutterstock: 12; Bruce Raynor/Shutterstock: 8; Tom Reichner/Shutterstock: 31 (right), 42; B.G. Smith/Shutterstock: 4; Debbie Steinhausser/Shutterstock: 7; Teri Virbickis/ Shutterstock: 30; U.S. Fish and Wildlife Service: 23 (right), 24; Wikimedia Commons: 53.